Little Xena's Amazing Day

This book is dedicated to Cynthia
and Joey Heaton, founders and owners
of Trinity Rescue. Without them,
there would be no Little Xena.

Credits:

Written by: Marcia Camp Johnson
Illustrated by: Peggie Daniel McGee

Printed in the United States of America

Rev. date: 03/08/2019

To order additional copies of this book, contact:
Xlibris
1-888-795-4274
www.Xlibris.com
Orders@Xlibris.com

It was a pretty April day filled with sunshine
when Little Xena, the miniature horse, was born.

1

Little Xena was so beautiful.

She was gray and white and had the
curliest mane you had ever seen.
Her little tail was white and fluffy.

Little Xena tried to stand up, like all baby ponies do when they are born.

But she could not stand up.

Her mommy, Tadpole, tried to help her stand up.

Finally, Little Xena stood up.

Tadpole looked at Little Xena's legs and hooves and realized something was wrong.

Little Xena's legs were crooked and her hooves were bent the wrong way.

Little Xena saw her mommy
Tadpole was worried.

"Oh no, Mommy. Will I be able to walk and run like
all the other ponies?" Little Xena asked.

Tadpole said, "We will find someone to help your legs and hooves get well so you can run and play with the other ponies. Do not be afraid, Little Xena."

Tadpole called for help and help came.

A special farm called Trinity Rescue came
to get Little Xena and Tadpole.
Trinity Rescue was a wonderful place
where all kinds of horses came
to become healthy.
Little Xena knew
she was at
the right place.

The great people at
Trinity Rescue arranged for Little
Xena to have surgery on her legs. They also
had special little boots made for her hooves
to help get them turned the right way.

In no time at all, Little Xena was walking. She worked hard every day to make her legs stronger.

She wore the boots on her hooves even though, sometimes they hurt a little bit.

Little Xena continued to exercise her legs and do all the things to make her stronger and stronger.

Soon she was able to play with the other ponies.

Then came the magic day.
Little Xena decided to try to run.

And oh, how she could run!

Her favorite friend was another miniature
horse named Oliver.

They loved being together all the time.

But not all the horses were like her friend Oliver. Some of the horses would not play with her because she could not run as fast as they could.

Other horses laughed at her because her legs and hooves looked different.

Little Xena became very sad.

But her friend Oliver was not going to let Xena be sad. He said, "Xena, it does not matter if you look different or cannot run as fast as the other horses. You can be anything you want to be."

"Thank you, Oliver", said Xena. "I am going to keep trying harder every day to practice my manners, be kind to everyone, and help the other horses see the good in me and not just my crooked legs."

And work hard she did! She was kind and respectful to everyone.

In fact, she was so full of love, when Trinity Rescue needed one of their horses to go on a visit to the Children's Hospital, guess who they picked?
Little Xena!

Xena was so happy she ran through the flowers in the pasture, kicking her back legs in the air.

The day arrived for Little Xena to go meet
the children at the Children's Hospital.

She picked a beautiful little pink outfit to wear for her special
visit. She even had cute pink boots on her little hooves.

All the way to the Children's Hospital, Little Xena was so happy. She felt like a princess. She could not help but be so proud of all her hard work and how SHE was chosen to be THE horse to represent Trinity Rescue and meet all the children.

When the horse trailer arrived at the Children's Hospital, Little Xena was holding her breath with excitement. She walked into the hospital holding her head so high, forgetting all about her crooked legs and hooves. It was time to meet the children.

Xena's first visit was with Will. She walked into his room with a big smile. Will smiled too. As Little Xena approached Will's bed, he reached out to Xena and asked, "May I please pet her?"
"Of course, you can, Will", said the nurse.

Will rubbed Little Xena's muzzle and
tickled her ears. Xena moved closer
to Will and laid her head on his bed
so he could touch her mane.
Will stroked her face and said,
"Oh Xena, I wish you could stay
with me all day."

Xena thought to herself,
"I do too, Will."

As Xena left Will's room, Will said,
"Xena you were brave when you had
your legs operated on. I am going
to be brave just like you."

Little Xena gave Will another big
smile and said goodbye so she could
see the other children.

The next stop was to see Sara. Sara was sitting in her wheelchair waiting for her visit from Little Xena.

When Xena came in the room, Sara's pretty blue eyes opened wide as they could. "Oh Xena", exclaimed Sara, "You are so beautiful!"

Sara had a pretty pink hairbrush in her hand. "May I please brush Xena's mane?" asked Sara. "Of course, you can, Sara", said the nurse.

Little Xena moved closer to Sara. Sara brushed Xena's mane and made it look so straight and pretty. Sara then took one of her own bows and tied it to Xena's mane. "You can have my bow, Little Xena. It makes you even prettier."

Xena smiled her biggest
smile of the day.
She nuzzled Sara
to say thank you and good bye.

As Xena was leaving Sara's room, Sara said,
"Little Xena, one day I'm going to walk and run just like you. Little Xena nodded her head to say,
"Yes, you will, Sara."

After many, many visits with the children,
it was time for Little Xena to return to her home.

All the children
had loved her.
None of the
children
had made
fun of her
legs or
laughed at the
way she walked.

Xena knew she had helped the children feel they could be
anything they wanted to be, just like Oliver had told her.

Little Xena returned to her home at Trinity Rescue that evening, tired but very, very happy. She had really made the children smile and helped them feel better.

"Yes, I am Different from other horses", Xena thought, "but I have a very special gift by being different. Now I know I have a great purpose in life and I can help make the world a kinder place."

As Little Xena closed her eyes to go to sleep,
she smiled one more time and said,
"What an AMAZING day!"

Marcia Camp Johnson, a LaGrange, Georgia native, has a long career in the life and health insurance profession. Marcia describes herself as "cause driven" and spends a lot of her spare- time volunteering. Her passions include animal rights, children in need, and veterans' support; helping to give a voice to those who often "can- not speak for themselves". Ms. Johnson is a graduate of the University of Alabama and the mother of a wonderful daughter. Published author of articles for magazines, this is her first children's book.

Peggie Daniel McGee grew up in the small town of Lagrange, Georgia in a loving family who supported and encouraged her passion for art. Before Peggie could read, she loved to go to the library with her older sisters and immerse herself in the "picture books". Working as a textile designer, Peggie never lost her love for children's books and animation. Recently retired, Peggie is enjoying using her creative energy to pursue her passion for fine art and illustration. With international recognition for her design work, this is Peggie's first foray into illustration.

Meet
Little Xena

Little Xena was brought to Trinity Rescue at 2 days old. Over the next six months, she made numerous trips to the University of Georgia School of Veterinary Medicine for surgeries and follow up appointments.